Determined to Be Free

NELSON MANDELA

by Jack L. Roberts

A Gateway Biography
The Millbrook Press
Brookfield, Connecticut

Library of Congress Cataloging-in-Publication Data
Roberts, Jack L.
Nelson Mandela: determined to be free / by Jack Roberts.
p.   cm. — (A Gateway biography)
Includes bibliographical references and index.
Summary: A biography of Nelson Mandela, his
lifelong struggle against the system of apartheid and
years of imprisonment followed by his 1994 victory
as South Africa's first black president.
ISBN 1-56294-558-0
1. Mandela, Nelson, 1918- —Juvenile literature.   2. Statesmen
—South Africa—Biography—Juvenile literature. [1. Mandela,
Nelson, 1918-   .   2. Civil rights workers.   3. Blacks—South
Africa—Biography.   4. Presidents—South Africa.   5. South
Africa—Race relations.]   I. Title.   II. Series.
DT1949.M35R63   1995
968.06'4'092—dc20   [B]   94-21519   CIP   AC

Published by The Millbrook Press, Inc.
2 Old New Milford Road
Brookfield, Connecticut 06804

Cover photograph courtesy of Wide World Photos
Cover background photograph courtesy of Ginger Giles

Photographs courtesy of AP/Wide World Photos: pp. 4, 15,
18, 21, 25, 28, 31, 38, 41 (both), 42; Impact Visuals: pp. 9
(Peter Auf Der Hyde), 22 (Eli Weinberg, IDAF); United
Nations: pp. 12 (photo 155283/Allen Tannenbaum), 35
(bottom, photo 155586); Reuters/Bettmann: p. 35 (top).

Nelson Mandela

Nelson Mandela has never stopped fighting for justice and equality for black South Africans.

Twelve-year-old *Rolihlahla* stood silently by his father's side in their tiny thatched hut near the Bashee River. The young tribal prince knew that this was an important day.

Rolihlahla's father was a poor but respected chief of the Tembu, one of many black African groups in the southeastern part of South Africa. But now this proud chief was sick, and certain he would die soon. So he had asked the paramount chief of the Tembu tribe to come to his family *kraal,* or farm.

The dying man wanted to make sure that Rolihlahla, his only son, would have a good education. He wanted to make sure that Rolihlahla would be raised to become a future chief of the Tembu.

Rolihlahla's father spoke softly to the paramount chief, asking him to take Rolihlahla to raise. "I am giving you this servant, Rolihlahla," he said. "I want you to make him what you would like him to be." Then he proudly added, "I can say from the way he speaks to his sisters and friends that his inclination is to help the nation."

Sadly, Rolihlahla's father did not live to see his

prediction come true. But fortunately for millions of people in South Africa and throughout the world, Rolihlahla's inclination was, indeed, to help the nation.

The young boy grew up to become better known throughout the world as Nelson Mandela, civil rights leader and hero to millions. He grew up to lead the struggle for justice and racial equality in South Africa. He became a beloved South African patriot whose struggle for freedom never weakened despite some twenty-seven years behind prison walls.

At various times during his life, Nelson Mandela has been a prince, a politician, and a prisoner. And on May 10, 1994, he became president of South Africa.

Through it all, he has been committed to one goal for himself and the millions of black South Africans: Nelson Mandela has always been a man determined to be free.

Nelson Rolihlahla Mandela was born on July 18, 1918, in southeastern South Africa to Nosekeni and

Henry Gadla Mandela. Like his father before him, the baby boy was given both an English name and a tribal one. His English-language name, Nelson, shows the influence of the British in South Africa. They once ruled all the tribes in the country. Rolihlahla means "stirring up trouble" in the African language of Xhosa (pronounced Cho-sa).

As a boy, Rolihlahla liked to sit around the open fire at night and listen to the elders tell stories of his homeland long before white people came to South Africa. "Then our people lived peacefully, under the democratic rule of their kings," Mandela later said. One of those kings was Nelson Rolihlahla Mandela's great-great-grandfather.

Rolihlahla also liked to watch and listen to the paramount chief conduct court. Other chiefs of the Tembu would bring their disputes before the paramount chief, who would listen to both sides. Rolihlahla was fascinated with the courtroom process and decided that one day he would like to become a lawyer.

Until he was twelve years old, Rolihlahla went to a white church school run by missionaries. One of his teachers could not pronounce his tribal name. So she decided he would be called by his first name, Nelson, and the name stuck.

Even though he had been born into a royal family, the family did not have much money. As a boy, Nelson wore hand-me-down clothes to school. Other children would laugh at him. But this didn't bother Nelson. He was happy just to be in school and to have an opportunity to learn so many new things.

When he was not in school, Nelson worked on the family kraal, helping with the plowing. He herded cattle in the pastures along the Bashee River. For fun, he hunted and played games with the other children in the village.

Thinking back on those days, Mandela once said, "I have the most pleasant recollections and dreams about my childhood."

In 1930, after his father died, Mandela left his mother and sisters in order to live with the paramount chief, as his father had wished. There, the teenager went to a Christian high school.

When Mandela was twenty years old, he enrolled in University College at Fort Hare, one of the few colleges that accepted black students. At

Nelson was born in this village. His relatives still keep a plot of land there for him.

Fort Hare, he met a student named Oliver Tambo, who would become a lifelong friend and freedom fighter along with Mandela. Together, they would spend long hours talking about how to gain more rights for black South Africans.

In college, by all accounts, Mandela was a popular young man. Tall and handsome, he enjoyed his social life and his studies.

In his third year of college, however, Nelson Mandela ran into some trouble. He was a member of the Students' Representative Council. The school authorities suddenly took away the organization's powers. Mandela and other students protested. As a result, he was suspended from school and sent home.

The paramount chief was very disappointed in Mandela. He decided it was time for the young man to get married and settle down. So, as was customary, the chief picked out a young woman for Mandela to marry.

Mandela did not want to get married, particularly to someone he hardly knew and didn't love. So he ran away to Johannesburg, the largest city in South Africa. He was twenty-two years old.

B*y the time* Mandela arrived in Johannesburg in 1941, there were more than 30 million people living in South Africa. Only 3 million of them were white Afrikaners. Yet the Afrikaners controlled the government.

This all-white government, or Parliament, as it was known, had passed some unjust laws. First, it passed a law that said only white people could vote in political elections. That left the blacks with no voice in the government.

Second, it passed a law known as the "pass system." This law required all Africans to have a special pass with them at all times. If they were stopped by the police and didn't have their passes, they could be arrested and put in jail.

Finally, the government gave 87 percent of the land to the whites, even though whites represented less than 12 percent of the population.

In Johannesburg, Mandela was shocked by what he discovered. Although the city was thriving and prosperous, Africans were not allowed to live there. They were instead forced to live in poor, overcrowded areas on the outskirts of town.

Mandela was shocked to see slums such as this one when he arrived in Johannesburg. Families lived in one-room shanties with dirt floors, no plumbing, and often little to eat.

For the first time in his life, Nelson Mandela saw the ugliness of segregation (the separation of the races). He also discovered what it meant to be a second-class citizen. For example, blacks were required to step off the sidewalk when a white person was passing.

It was during this time that Mandela realized how he would like to serve his people. As he once explained it, he decided to make his own humble contribution to their struggle for freedom.

In Johannesburg, Mandela met a man named Walter Sisulu, who owned a small real-estate agency. Sisulu gave Mandela a job. At the same time, he encouraged Mandela to finish his college education and later helped him get a part-time job in a law firm.

In 1944, Mandela married Sisulu's cousin, Evelyn Ntoko Mase. She worked as a nurse, while Mandela began studying to become a lawyer at the University of Witwatersrand.

Sisulu was a member of a political organization called the African National Congress (ANC). Soon, Mandela and his friend Tambo joined the organization as well.

The ANC was dedicated to bringing about social change in South Africa. It wanted to achieve equal rights for all Africans. But Mandela and his friends felt that the group wasn't doing enough. They felt the ANC needed some new ideas.

So Mandela and Sisulu and some of their friends formed a group within the ANC called the Congress Youth League. The purpose of the Youth League was to end discrimination throughout South Africa. They wanted all Africans to have full rights as citizens. Most important, they wanted every African adult to have the right to vote. It would be nearly fifty years, however, before they would achieve that goal.

In 1948 a new Afrikaner National Party came into power. This conservative all-white government passed what it called the laws of apartheid (pronounced apart-hate). Apartheid means "apartness" or "separateness." The new laws of apartheid further reduced the rights of the African people.

One of these laws was the Population Registration Act. Under this law, every South African was

Members of the ANC, including Sisulu (right), are arrested in 1952 for refusing to follow the laws of apartheid.

classified as a member of one of four races: white, Colored (the South African term for people of mixed race), Asian, or African. Africans and Asians could not vote at all. And Coloreds could vote only for white candidates.

Another law said that nonwhites could not be on the streets after 11:00 P.M. One night, Mandela's Youth League and other anti-apartheid volunteers decided to defy, or go against, this law. Mandela led this group into the street after the 11:00 P.M. curfew. All were immediately arrested. It was the first time Nelson Mandela was put in jail. It would not be his last.

The shameful policies of apartheid meant that it was all right for whites to treat blacks as if they were less than human. Mandela called apartheid an "insane policy" and vowed to fight against it.

The Youth League created what it called a Programme of Action. This new program encouraged many acts of civil disobedience as a way to protest the new policies.

One of their first acts of civil disobedience was a National Work Stoppage Day. The Youth League planned this work stoppage for May Day 1950.

More than half the workforce refused to go to work. Instead, they gathered in town to protest the government's policies.

Then tragedy struck. A riot broke out in one of the towns. The police fired into the crowd and eighteen Africans were killed. "That day," Mandela later said, "was a turning point in my life."

Toward the end of 1950, Mandela was elected national president of the Youth League. Suddenly, he was becoming an important national leader of the anti-apartheid movement.

At about this time, the white government tried another way of controlling or stopping the anti-apartheid movement. Africans who ignored the apartheid policies were punished by banning. A person who was banned was prevented from doing many things—sometimes for a few months, sometimes for years. When banned, people could not leave their towns. They could not be out after dark or on the weekends. They could not be quoted in a newspaper or magazine. And they could not be in the same room with more than three people at

Race riots, such as this one in Johannesburg, were common.
The police beat many people, including women and children,
and sometimes shot into the crowd and killed them.

any one time. If a person broke a ban, he or she could be sent to prison.

Beginning in 1952, Mandela was repeatedly banned, the first time for taking part in a protest against unjust laws. When one ban expired, the government would soon find a reason to issue another one.

The bans made Mandela and others feel like criminals. As he put it, "I was made, by the law, a criminal, not because of what I had done, but because of what I stood for, because of what I thought, because of my conscience."

In 1955 the ANC and other political groups held an important conference. The people at the conference voted to adopt a document called the Freedom Charter. This Charter said, in part: "We, the people of South Africa, declare for all our country and the world to know that South Africa belongs to all who live in it, black and white, and that no government can justly claim authority unless it is based on the will of all the people."

Since Mandela was banned during the time of the conference, he was not supposed to attend the meeting. But he couldn't resist, and he went anyway. A year later Mandela and 155 other political leaders who had attended this conference were arrested for treason.

Their trial, which became known as the Treason Trial, lasted for five years. During that time, Mandela was out on bail. Finally, in 1961, Mandela and the others were found not guilty.

By now, Mandela and Evelyn had two young boys, Madiba (called Thembi), who was born in 1945, and Makgatho, born in 1950. (A baby girl named Makaziwe was born in 1948, but died before she was a year old.) Later, in 1954, they would have another daughter whom they would also name Makaziwe (known as Maki).

By the end of 1955, Mandela's political activities were taking a toll on his family life. As a leader in the ANC, Mandela spent a great deal of time away from home at protests and demonstrations and meetings. Evelyn wanted a more normal home life. Eventually, the couple realized that they had grown apart and got a divorce.

In 1956, Mandela met a beautiful young woman named Winifred Nomzamo Madikizela. Two years later, in June 1958, they were married. They had

Nelson Mandela (right) and two other men are brought by bus to stand trial in August 1958. By this time, blacks were starting to look to Mandela as an important leader.

Winnie and Nelson Mandela on their wedding day.

two daughters: Zindziswa (Zindzi) and Zenani (Zeni). Winnie Mandela soon became her husband's partner in the struggle for freedom and a civil rights leader in her own right.

For twenty years, Mandela believed that blacks could achieve their freedom through nonviolence. And he worked to bring about change through nonviolent acts. Then, in 1960, an event occurred that had a profound effect on Mandela. It was an event that would change his opinion about nonviolence forever.

On March 21, 1960, a group of peaceful protesters in a town called Sharpeville marched to the police station without their passes. With fists raised, they shouted "Amandla!" which means "Power!" in Xhosa, the language spoken by many black South Africans.

Some of the protesters threw stones at the police. Suddenly, without warning, the police opened fire, shooting and killing sixty-nine black protesters, including eight women and ten children. Most of them were shot in the back.

The unnecessary brutality was hard for anyone to understand or to accept. The African National Congress called for a day of mourning for those who had been killed. And on March 28, almost all of the country's nonwhite workers stayed home.

Until that day, Mandela and others had worked for racial equality through nonviolence. But now they had to admit that they had not succeeded in achieving their goals. Perhaps it was time to answer violent acts with violence.

This decision did not come easily. As Mandela later said, "It was only when all other forms of resistance were no longer open to us that we turned to armed struggle." Then, he added, "If the government reaction is to crush by naked force our nonviolent struggle, we will have to reconsider our tactics. In my mind, we are closing a chapter on this question of nonviolent policy."

In order to carry out their new tactics, Mandela and other leaders formed a new organization called *Umkhonto we Sizwe* (Spear of the Nation). This was a military wing of the African National Congress, and Mandela became its first commander.

Dead and wounded lie on the ground in Sharpeville on March 21, 1960, after police fired on a crowd. Never before had so many protesters been killed.

The group discussed various actions they could take to fight apartheid, including terrorist acts. Finally they decided they would try to destroy government buildings or property. These acts are known as sabotage. Mandela was in favor of sabotage as a way to fight apartheid for one important reason. As he explained, "Sabotage did not involve loss of life and it offered the best hope for future race relations." In fact, from the beginning, the members of Spear of the Nation were given strict orders: No one was to be injured or killed in their acts of sabotage.

Soon Umkhonto we Sizwe distributed leaflets explaining its new position. In his talks with his people, Mandela said, "The time comes in the life of any nation when there remain only two choices: submit or fight. That time has now come to South Africa."

At about this same time, the police issued a warrant for Mandela's arrest. So, in order to run this new group, the civil rights leader went "underground." For the next seventeen months, the police were not able to find him. He had left the country using a fake passport. He was living in Algeria, where he studied how to better carry out acts of sabotage.

At one point during this period, Mandela issued a statement to the press. He called for everyone to continue the fight against apartheid. "Only through hardship, sacrifice, and militant struggle can freedom be won," he said. "The struggle is my life. I will continue fighting for freedom until the end of my days."

On *August 5, 1962,* the police finally caught Mandela and charged him with two crimes. The first was encouraging a strike. The second was leaving the country without a valid passport.

When he was brought to trial, Mandela challenged the right of the court to hear his case. "I consider myself neither legally nor morally bound to obey laws made by a parliament in which I have no representation." Nevertheless, the trial continued, and on October 25, Mandela was found guilty. He was sent to a maximum security prison on Robben Island, 7 miles (11 kilometers) off the coast of Cape Town.

A crowd shows support for Mandela during his 1962 trial.

In the fall of 1963, Mandela was brought back to Pretoria for another trial. This time he was accused of sabotage and trying to overthrow the government. Walter Sisulu and other leaders of Spear of the Nation were also charged with the same crime.

The trial began on October 9, 1963. When asked how he wanted to plead, Mandela answered: "The government should be in the dock [standing here], not me. I plead not guilty."

On June 11, 1964, after eight long months on trial, Mandela was convicted. Before being sentenced, he was given a chance to speak to the court. "During my lifetime," he said, "I have dedicated myself to the struggle of the African people. I have fought against white domination, and I have fought against black domination. I have cherished the ideal of a democratic and free society in which all persons live together in harmony and with equal opportunities. It is an ideal which I hope to live for and to achieve. But if needs be, it is an ideal for which I am prepared to die."

In his powerful and moving speech that day, Mandela also told the court that blacks were not a "separate breed." Like people everywhere, he said, blacks simply want the opportunity to earn a living and raise a family in peace. But most of all they want freedom in their own land. With that freedom, Mandela said, comes human dignity.

Mandela spoke for more than four hours. Yet, it took the judge only three minutes to deliver his verdict: guilty. And on June 11, 1964, Mandela and the other convicted prisoners were sentenced to life in prison.

As they were led from the courtroom to the waiting van that would take them to Robben Island Prison, Mandela and the others looked at the crowd and cried: "Amandla!"

At Robben Island, Mandela was put into a small cell that was only 7 feet (2 meters) square. There was not so much as a cot on the floor. For the first nine years, he also had no hot water.

Each day, he and the other prisoners were forced to work long hours in the lime quarry. Their job was to break up rocks in the quarry, a back-breaking, exhausting job. Years later, Mandela suf-

Police hold back a crowd protesting the decision on Mandela's case. He was found guilty and sent to prison, where he would remain for the next twenty-seven and a half years.

fered problems with his eyes as a result of the dust from the quarry.

From the beginning, Mandela fought to improve the prison conditions. Initially, his fight was for the simplest of things, such as better food or the right to exercise.

Year after year, he labored on. At first, his wife Winnie could visit him only twice a year—and then only for thirty minutes each time. He was not allowed to see his children at all. Years later, when his son Thembi was killed in a car crash, he was not even allowed out to go to the funeral.

Gradually, Mandela won for himself and the other prisoners certain "privileges," such as a blanket to keep warm at night and hot water for a shower. But life was still difficult. As he explained, "South Africa's prisons are intended to cripple us so that we should never again have the strength and courage to pursue our ideals."

During these years, the government tried to get the people of South Africa to forget about Mandela. It banned the publication of all of his earlier speeches or interviews. It also did not allow any photograph of Mandela to be published. Yet his popularity continued to grow. People throughout the world began demanding his release.

Meanwhile, life for South Africans was becoming even more harsh. People could be arrested by the police for almost any reason. They would often disappear forever. Even Winnie Mandela, who had become an anti-apartheid leader in her own right, was harassed and jailed many times. Once she spent eighteen months in solitary confinement.

By the mid-1970s, life in prison had improved somewhat. Mandela was allowed to take courses in economics. He also studied the Afrikaner language. And he and the other prisoners were allowed to see a movie once a month.

In September 1978, a new prime minister came to power. His name was P. W. Botha. Botha began talking about releasing Mandela, but only on certain conditions—all of which Nelson Mandela turned down.

In April 1982, Mandela was transferred to Pollsmoor Maximum Security Prison in Pretoria. There, life was somewhat better for this civil rights leader who was now sixty-four years old. He was able to have English-language newspapers. But he was still not allowed to be quoted by the press.

On January 31, 1985, Botha made a startling announcement. He said he would release Mandela on one condition. Mandela had to promise that he would never again be involved in acts of violence against the government.

Mandela's response was simple and direct. "Only free men can negotiate," he said. "I cannot sell my birthright, nor am I prepared to sell the birthright of the people to be free." Instead, Mandela demanded that his release from prison be unconditional. He particularly wanted a guarantee that he would be allowed to travel throughout his country and the world.

In 1986 there was again speculation that Nelson Mandela would soon be released from prison. Even *The Washington Post* carried a headline that read: "Winnie Mandela Expects Her Husband's Release." Winnie was thrilled with the thought that her husband might soon be free. "The whole country will turn out to welcome him," she predicted. "The return of the people's Messiah. Everybody

Prime Minister P. W. Botha is addressing the nation on television. Life for blacks did not improve while he was in office.

Mourners carry the coffins of people who were shot by the police at a gathering on International Day for the Elimination of Racial Discrimination. This day was the anniversary of the Sharpeville massacre.

will be in the streets. Everything will come to a standstill." But, sadly, his release never came.

Releasing Nelson Mandela from prison was a complicated matter. As Winnie explained, "How do they release Mandela into an apartheid society, knowing he will not abide by its rules? How do they release him while the ANC is still banned, knowing he will ignore the ban and take up where he left off as its leader?"

In August 1988, Mandela came down with tuberculosis and almost died in Pollsmoor Prison. After he recovered, he was transferred to the Victor Verster prison farm, 40 miles (64 kilometers) northeast of Cape Town. Considering what he had been through, this was almost like living in a resort. He was placed in what had previously been the warden's home—it even had a swimming pool.

Soon afterward, in November 1988, the government once again offered to release him. But again he said no. He insisted that five other men who had been arrested with him be released first, including Walter Sisulu.

In February 1989, Botha resigned as prime minister due to illness. And in September 1989, a new man took control of the government. His name was F. W. de Klerk. Everyone believed that de Klerk would bring about some important political changes. They were right.

In December 1990, de Klerk told the press, "Apartheid cannot succeed. The National Party has now accepted that all South Africans will permanently share power."

Then, on February 2, 1990, President de Klerk lifted the thirty-year ban on the ANC and said that no more hangings would take place in South Africa pending a review of the death penalty. He also announced that he was soon going to release Mandela unconditionally.

When South Africans heard the news, they were thrilled. "What he said has certainly taken my breath away," said Archbishop Desmond Tutu, the first black to head South Africa's Anglican Church. "His speech was incredible."

Finally, on a sunny Sunday morning, on February 11, 1990, a silver sedan drove through the gates of Victor Verster Prison and stopped. A tall, distinguished-looking gentleman got out of the car and waved to the crowd. Thousands of people cheered,

Winnie and Nelson Mandela walk hand-in-hand after his long-awaited release from prison in 1990.

shouting "Amandla!" After twenty-seven years, six months, and one week in prison, Nelson Mandela was free. He was seventy-one years old.

The hardships that Mandela endured during those years are hard to imagine. "Every day behind bars was a battle for dignity," he has said. "My fate is not one I would wish upon even the worst of my enemies. It is a cruelty to which no decent society would want to expose its citizens."

Soon after his release, Mandela renounced the use of violence. At the same time, de Klerk repealed, or canceled, many of the laws of apartheid.

For the next four years, Mandela and de Klerk met many times to discuss the future of their country. "We have no alternative but to work together to bring about a democratic South Africa," Mandela told the world.

On April 13, 1992, Mandela announced to the press that he and Winnie were separating, after thirty-four years of marriage. It was a very sad day for Mandela, who told the press, "My love for her remains undiminished."

In trying to explain the breakup, Mandela said that he and Winnie strongly disagreed on some very important political issues. As a result, these differences created a lot of tension between them.

In November 1993, Mandela and de Klerk agreed to set up the country's first free election. The new government would rule for five years, during which time a new constitution would be written.

This agreement did not come easily. Political violence during this time resulted in the deaths of more than ten thousand people.

Nevertheless, in recognition of their remarkable accomplishments, in December 1993 the leaders shared a great honor. They were awarded the Nobel Peace Prize.

Throughout his life, Nelson Mandela has had one purpose. He has struggled and fought for a free, democratic South Africa. He has fought for a country in which all people can vote.

That goal was finally achieved on April 29, 1994. On that historic day, Nelson Mandela—a man who

Left: F. W. de Klerk and Nelson Mandela receiving the UNESCO peace prize in Paris for their efforts to end segregation in South Africa. Below: Before the first free elections in South Africa, the country was torn apart by violence between blacks and between blacks and whites. This crowd wants to stop the ANC from taking control of the new government.

Nelson Mandela, his hands clenched in victory, rises to give his first speech as president of South Africa.

had been born a prince but who lived most of his life as a political prisoner—was elected president of South Africa in the first open election ever held in that country.

Yet the troubles in South Africa are not over. "Our country will never be free until all our people live in brotherhood, enjoying rights and opportunities," Mandela has said.

And so, today, Nelson Mandela continues his lifelong fight for justice, equality, and human dignity for all people determined to be free.

Important Dates

■■■■■■■■

1918   Nelson Rolihlahla Mandela is born on July 18.

1938   Mandela enrolls in University College at Fort Hare.

1944   Nelson Mandela, Oliver Tambo, and Walter Sisulu form the Congress Youth League, a branch of the African National Congress (ANC).

1944   Mandela marries Evelyn Ntoko Mase; they divorce in 1957 after having four children.

1948   The Afrikaner National Party wins control of the government; policies of apartheid begin.

1950   Mandela is elected president of the ANC's Youth League.

1952	Mandela is arrested for breaking curfew laws on June 26.
1956	On December 5, Mandela and other ANC leaders are arrested for "high treason"; they are acquitted and freed in 1961.
1958	On June 14, Mandela marries Winifred Nomzamo Madikizela; they have two daughters.
1960	Black protesters are massacred in Sharpeville on March 21.
1961	Mandela and others form *Umkhonto we Sizwe* (Spear of the Nation); Mandela goes into hiding.
1962	Mandela is captured and sentenced to five years in prison for leading African workers in a strike.
1963	While in prison, Nelson Mandela is charged with sabotage.
1964	On June 11, Mandela is sentenced to "life in prison plus five years."
1989	De Klerk becomes president of South Africa.
1990	Mandela is released from prison on February 11.
1992	Mandela and de Klerk are awarded the UNESCO Peace Prize.
1993	Mandela and de Klerk are awarded the Nobel Peace Prize.
1994	On April 29, Nelson Mandela is elected president of South Africa. He is inaugurated on May 10.

Further Reading

Denenberg, Barry. *Nelson Mandela.* New York: Scholastic Inc., 1991.

Feinberg, Brian. *Nelson Mandela.* New York: Chelsea House Publishers, 1991.

Hargrove, J. *Nelson Mandela: South Africa's Silent Voice of Protest.* Chicago: Childrens Press, 1989.

Pogrund, Benjamin. *Nelson Mandela.* Milwaukee, Wisc.: Gareth Stevens, Inc., 1992.

Tames, Richard. *Nelson Mandela.* New York: Franklin Watts, 1991.

Index

Page numbers in *italics* refer to illustrations.

African National Congress, 13–14, 19, 20, 24, 36, 37
Afrikaner National Party, 14, 37
Afrikaners, 11
Apartheid, 14, 16, 26, 27, 37, 39

Banning, 17, 19
Botha, P. W., 33, 34, *35*, 36

Congress Youth League, 14, 16, 17

de Klerk, F. W., 37, 39, 40, *41*

Freedom Charter, 19

Johannesburg, 10, *12*

Mandela, Evelyn Ntoko Mase, 13, 20
Mandela, Henry Gadla, 7
Mandela, Madiba (Thembi), 20, 32
Mandela, Makaziwe (Maki), 20
Mandela, Makgatho, 20
Mandela, Nelson, *4, 38, 41*

Mandela, Nelson
(*continued*)
  African National
    Congress and, 13–14, 20
  banning of, 19
  birth of, 6–7
  childhood of, 5–8
  children of, 20, 23
  Congress Youth League
    and, 14, 16, 17
  education of, 7–8, 10, 13
  in hiding, 26–27
  marriages of, 13, 20
  nonviolent policy of, 23,
    24
  as president of South
    Africa, 6, 40, *42*, 43
  in prison, 6, 16, 27, 30,
    32–34, 36, 37, 39
  release from prison, 37,
    39
  sabotage and, 26, 27
  trials of, 20, *21*, 27, *28*,
    29–30
  Umkhonto we Sizwe
    (Spear of the Nation)
    and, 24, 26, 29
Mandela, Nosekeni, 6
Mandela, Winifred
  Nomzamo Madikizela, 20,
  22, 23, 32–34, 36, *38*,
  39–40
Mandela, Zenani (Zeni), 23
Mandela, Zindziswa
  (Zindzi), 23

National Work Stoppage
  Day (1950), 16–17
Nobel Peace Prize, 40

Pollsmoor Maximum
  Security Prison, 33, 36
Population Registration
  Act, 14, 16
Programme of Action, 16

Robben Island, 27, 30
Rolihlahla (*see* Mandela,
  Nelson)

Sabotage, 26, 27
Segregation, 11, 13
Sharpeville massacre, 23,
  25
Sisulu, Walter, 13, *15*, 29, 36

Tambo, Oliver, 10, 13
Tembu tribe, 5
Treason Trial, 20, *21*
Tutu, Desmond, 37

Umkhonto we Sizwe (Spear
  of the Nation), 24, 26, 29
University College, Fort
  Hare, 8, 10
University of
  Witwatersrand, 13

Victor Verster Prison, 36,
  37
Voting rights, 14